SUBAM

JOSEPH ADAMA

Joseph Adama

CONTENTS

Joseph Adama

1
JAKE'S STORY

My name is Jake Stalk and in "fourteen hours, Subam will be dead." The reign of President Subam, has been one disaster after another. It all started, with the bombing of "The Brooklyn Bridge" and a small group of terrorists from Palestine, who had been funded by Hamas and Iran, attached "bombs" to The Brooklyn Bridge. When the bombs were detonated, 6,000 people were killed. The current administration at that time, had very little answers and even less solutions, on how to prevent something like this, from happening again.

The American people, became increasingly fearful, to even live their lives. Always anticipating the next terrorist attack. The anger towards the ever lacking administration, grew more and more each day. So much so, that during the election season, people across the country, refused to vote for or even to accept, a Republican or Democratic candidate, for president. That's when a smooth talking man, from "The Communists Party," came forward, Sen. James Subam.

During The Campaign, Subam asked, *"Can a nation be free, if it oppresses other nations? No, it can't."* He then told the American people... *"We were attacked because of our social excess and very much, because of our support, for Israel. You see, the Capitalist Jews and those who follow them, they are the ones to blame for the horrible attack perpetrated, you see. The Palestinian people, were only defending themselves from constant attacks, committed by the Jews and those greedy money lovers who follow, you see..."*

Sen. Subam continued as I watched these useful idiots applaud and cheer, my mind went backwards, in a way as I sat watching his campaign speech from the recliner in my living room, Sen. Subam continued by...

"Socialism will meet the needs of the great majority of our people and lay the basis, for solving our social economic and most of all, our environmental problems." To my surprise, the majority of the American people bought it. "Hook line and sinker."

President Hannity tried desperately, to stop the United States from making the worst decision, "in our Nation's History." As he put it and I agreed with President Hannity, but the will of the American people, was too strong. On January 20, 2020 James Subam was sworn in as the 46th president of the United States of America. After which, President Subam wasted no time, imposing his rule.

Subam took complete control of people's private land and locking anyone up that disagreed. Subam then put drones in the sky. The drones, flew night and day, watching us. Any person brave enough, to speak out against President Subam and what he was doing, was thrown in prison indefinitely.

"My friend Ivan Valentin," seen what was happening and he didn't like it, to say the least. I remember Ivan telling me, on the day Subam was elected, that he would start a war with him if necessary. "Aren't you talking treason?" I asked. Ivan replied, "Sometimes the traitor turns out being the most patriotic one of them all." He then grinned, before walking out.

The last time I seen Ivan, was on the TV. As he stood in front of a firing wall, he then gave the firing squad a salute and he was gone. My friend Ivan died as a hero, at the age of 29. He was killed by cowards yet still, I didn't fight. No! I'm ashamed to say it but I submitted and told myself, that a 56-year-old Cuban, wasn't any match for the US Army and God forbid, that Subam learned about my Jewish blood.

Hell, I can't raise an army. As I thought to myself, "No! Ivan was brave but he was also stupid." Much like most of America, I just stood by and let my Country be taken away from me. The United States was replaced by a "Soviet like Police State." Subam was ruthless, with those who crossed him. Even having the Vice President tarred, feathered and executed, on The White House Lawn.

Two years after his Presidency, the rumors surrounding the incident, involving Vice President Andronikos Archelaus, was that Vice President Archelaus, made a comment about Subam's tie. That alone, caused the humiliation and execution of the late Vice President. For that reason, I've decided that I would just lay low and try not to bring on any, unwanted attention.

I wasn't about to pull an Ivan... What good would it do me or my wife, Isabella Stalk Castro or my son, Diego Stalk Juan Castro, to see me standing against a wall, waiting to be killed? No! My family doesn't deserve to see that. I told myself, that we would just try and live our lives, best as possible and we did. We lived an almost decent life, for six years. On the day of January 23, 2028 Subam's police came to my house, killed my wife and took my son. Now, "the eighth year anniversary" of my friend Ivan's death, I will finish what he has started.

I just wish I would have woken up sooner... Shit! I should have taken my family out of here, six fucking years ago, when I seen the Vice President murdered live on TV. Man that S.O.B Subam sure loves an audience. I couldn't tell you the number of people, President Subam has executed, live from The White House for the past, eight years. Now, finally after tonight, Subam's reign of terror, will come, to an end! I've acquired a fake identification, with the help of my fallen comrade, Carl's Ex-girlfriend, "Natalia." She has been more, than helpful, in my quest to end, Subam and with him, his "progressive counter parts."

As I look down at my watch, I see I have 13 hours remaining. I know, I have too move quick but I must also, be smart. I only have one chance, to get this right. I can only pray, that the fake diplomat papers, Carl's Ex-Natalia, acquired, works long enough, too put an end to Subam along with, other big players, in his new progressive order.

After I kill Subam, I plan too set a bomb, using tripwire packed with enough explosives, too leave a crater, the size of Popigai, in Siberia but first thing's first, I need to get inside, The White House. Thanks to Natalia, I've acquired a diplomatic meeting, with President Subam. All I can do now, is hope, Natalia's man on the inside, is as good, as she claims he is. Shit, as long as he can get me in, without suspicion, just long enough, to get the job done. God knows the chance of getting out alive, is slim to none and that's at my, best case scenario.

My plan is quite simple, after I enter The White House, I will have precisely, ten minutes, too shoot Subam, set the bomb and make my escape. All I have too do now, is wait for Natalia to contact me, with details about meeting her man, on the inside. One final look at my watch before I rest, tells me, all will take place in less, than 13 hours…

I awoken by my ringing cell, I answer to Natalia's soft, *Eastern European, accent.* *"Jake are you alone?"* Of course, what's wrong? *"My contact, he is dead now. I fear, President Subam's "Cheka," has information about you and our plan."* What? Natalia, how the Hell, did this happen? *"I am sorry Jake, but you may, be in danger."* Just like that, before I could even finish my thought, I heard Subam's police banging at my door. I then, quickly grabbed my gun, realizing my options, I head for the window. Jumping through the window, I land on the grass, on the side of my house. I hear Subam's police yelling at me, to stop. As I duck into the alley, they begin to shoot at me.

2
DIEGO'S STORY

My name, is Diego Stalk Castro. I'm telling you my story, from behind a cell inside of one of Subam's, execution camps. I will be dead soon, this I know. How I got here, I must start from the beginning, if you are to understand... You see, for years the Communists and Socialists politicians, have been infiltrating both, Democratic and Republican parties.

The first openly Marxist Politician, ran for President against then, President Fredrik Hannity, in the 2016 election. "Clenching" the Democratic nominee, receiving more than enough delegates and if not for such out spoken voices, such as *Glenn Beck, Rush Limbaugh* and of course, President Hannity, exposing the Marxist, Ben David French, for the dark tyrant, Ben French would have been, if elected.

Sure, *"The Vladstorian Post,"* did the best they could, to try and clean up their Candidate's image but thanks to the Conservative Commentators and in a large part, Marxist Ben Frenchs own words. Hell, his own campaign manager, none other than, *The Vladstorian Post* Bob Cesar's, had been caught teaching third graders about, *"Mao Sa Tung"* and how great, the Communist Dictator, was and for the first time, that I'm aware of, The Democrats, were humiliated and shown, for the "Mao lovers" that they were and with that, President Hannity, was over whelming, Re-elected and the American people were safe, for another four years...

With the bombing of The Brooklyn Bridge, the people were scared and becoming, evermore fearful. The Communists didn't waste anytime, taking advantage of the crisis, by giving us, Sen. James Subam. When Subam was elected in 2020, the people cheered. One month later and the people were in mourning. Subam seized all the food from the stores and rationed out, small portions. Each month, Subam would bring in trucks of food. Dishing out small sacks, to each person.

The food we received from Subam's goon's, was said to last us a month. It obviously did not because if it had, then 50,000 people wouldn't have starved to death, just eight months after his election. I remember, my dad's friend Ivan saying, that Subam would starve us, too keep us weak and dependent, to the government.

I wish Ivan was still alive, so I could tell him, just how right he really was. Sitting in cell 871, listening to the rats and to the other political prisoners, whine and scream, at our captors, just basically waiting to die. As I hear the screams, I wonder, why and how people could vote for a progressive. Being a damn naive people, is what killed us as a free nation. If only the American people, fully knew their history, then they would have known their future.

As easily as it's said about those, who voted for Subam and his late, vice president, the very liberal Andronikos Archelaus, it can be said about me, *"Stupidity is bliss, until you're chained, at the leg, with a boot, on your throat."* You see, I wasn't old enough to vote during Subam's run, being just 14. If I was 18, when that evil son of a bitch ran, I would have voted for the Communist Democratic Ticket. So yes, being naive and flat out ignorant people, is what killed our country.

244 years after we first won our independence. Now, as I sit here, I truly understand George Washington, when he told his men that, these were the times that try men's soul's. Well, it was really Thomas Pain, who said that but Washington acted on it more intensely. Shit! I'm nothing like the Founders. I didn't stand up, to that bastard Subam, until it was too late, to fight or do anything else, for that matter.

I should have listened to Ivan but I didn't and all I can do now, is wait to die. Maybe, if there were more people out there like Ivan, or if the American people would have learned, the true history of The Founder's, even the words of former President Hannity, could and would have saved us. If only we had listened but we didn't and I believe, ironic would best describe a nation born, by resisting Socialism, that later dies, by the iron fist of Socialism, because "the once Great Nation."

The Nation, that crushed tyranny wherever it showed its ugly face, sometimes by force but at most times example, became lazy and fell asleep. As a country, we didn't see the beast as it came to our shore, nor did we pay attention when the beast knocked at our door. No! We all stayed in our slumbering state, in all stages of mankind. These things are known to repeat as it does throughout all time. What is true now, has always been because Politicians can talk smooth and that they do but when you put far too much trust, into anyone but you, I think it is safe to say, that your doomed because the government is here to take care of you.

Joseph Adama

3

PALE FACE'S STORY

Hello there, wherever you might be in this "New World Order," we all seem to be inside. My name is Pale Face Eagleheart. I grew up on the "Chippewa Reservation," here in California. When Subam first ran for president, he talked allot about giving honour, back to the Native people. He spoke, about the conditions, being horrible on most, if not all Native Reservations. *"When elected, I will bring pride back to your people! No longer, will your sick go without proper care! No longer, will we put in use, The Failed Policies, of our Nation's History! With me as President, The Nation of America, will be ours, for all times!"*

Subam proclaimed and we all bought his lies. That demon, known as President James Subam, was elected with over 90 percent, of the Native vote. Once in office, president Subam used the "bombings of the Brooklyn Bridge," as an excuse, to round up my people along with many others, forced into hard labor and for some, even death camps. I've been on the run, from such a fate, for five years now. I have not eluded Subam's police, simply by luck. If not for my aid, I would be dead, times over.

Natalia has been more than helpful. If not for her, I can't think about where I'd be. In 2023, Wednesday the 14th of July, I tried stopping one of that bastard's police, from "shooting a little girl." I'm sorry to say, that I tried in vane. She was six years old and they murdered her. For trying to prevent the atrocity, I was imprisoned, locked up in one of "Subam's Hard Labor

9

Camps." That's when I first met Natalia. The little Russian girl, I would later come to know, as Natalia. Natalia, has been working as a "Christian Missionary," offering prayer and counselling to the condemned men.

As I watched her sitting with the men, guarding them in prayer, I really admired the Maiden's strong courage and bravery. She would enter the prison each day alone, bringing comfort and hope, to and otherwise, hopeless place. All the while, having Subam's perverted guards, on her every step of the way. The guards have great hate, towards her Religious views. It wasn't until I learned who she truly was, that I understood why she would put herself in such danger, from one guard in particular, "Mr. Rue Navarre, Jr."

Navarre Jr. was always very offensive. Making jesters at her, constantly grabbing her butt. The sick Mr. Navarre Jr. was also, extremely racist. Sometimes, even spitting in the faces of black prisoners, as they sat and prayed with the "very mysterious," Natalia. Natalia would try her best, to act like the guard's actions, did not bother her but I'm sure they must have. Natalia first approached me, asking if I would like to pray. "Hello, would you like to ask the Lord for guidance?" No. I replied. "Is your God, going to reach down and take me out of this place?" What's your name, sir? Pale Face. Okay, Pale Face, I know you're suffering… Yeah, I'm sure! I yelled. Hey! Pale Face, come back! I heard her hollering for me to stop and come back, As I continued, walking back to my cell.

My cellmate, "George Lee Baxter," was standing in the doorway, running a pick through his very short, blonde hair. George was one of those, pumped up health nuts or at least he was, before being brought here. "Hey, Pale Face, Mr. Navarre Jr. said he needed to inform us, that we're going to be transferred to another work camp." When did he speak with you? Well, by speak… If you mean, when did the son of a whore and two of his flunkie's, rushed in our cell, beating me with their night sticks, before letting me know, that the two of us, along with a few others, were going to be moved, to another, Work Camp? They beat you? George showed me the welts and bruises across his ribs and back.

Later that night, I just sat in my bed, in disbelief at where I was.

Disbelief, at what happened to my country. A once great nation, in which anyone could be anything, they dreamed. Now most Americans are rotting in that bastard Subam's, Prison Camps or at best, living in the streets, like rats. I sat up the whole night crying. Every damn thing that had happened to me, my country and the spirit of America, it all just hit me at once.

The next morning, I figured it out, *"The Constitution, that very wisely divided the government, into three separate units, against any one branch usurping power. The Constitution was made irrelevant. An old tiered document, that had no real bearings, in today's world. James Subam ran a 24-hour commercial campaign, driving his twisted message home."*

That damn son of a bitch, used propaganda in such a way, that even Woodrow Wilson would be made to blush. Subam covered the walls of schools and businesses, with his sick propaganda posters. With zero support from the American people, Subam passed what he called, *"The Protected Free Speech Act 441B,"* which banned any books or person for that matter, that President Subam felt, was inappropriate or contradictory, to his damn message. That prick Subam twisted history, better than Adolf Hitler and Woodrow Wilson combined. Turning our beloved Founder's into angry, racist, he used what he called, his "Revisionism," to change America for the better. That's how we got here. The March towards Socialism, started with the promise of safety, through Collectivism and it will end, with the loss of any free thought.

Before George and I were transported, I looked for Natalia in her usual spot, where she would sit and pray with inmates, whoms crimes were nothing more, than having free thought. Because as it says across the walls of this place, *"Freedom is slavery. Hard work is the path to everlasting joy."* It was with a very thin pale Jew, that I had seen her. The Jew had his small face buried, in her long beautiful hair, as she sang silent night.

Then before I approached them, two guards came up, grabbing the Jew. They dragged the poor man into the execution room. Natalia hollered at the young Jewish man. "Be strong!" As I approached Natalia, she turned and looked at me, with tears, in her beautiful, blue eye's. Reaching over, I put my arm around her, as I pulled her into me, she whispered. *"One day, there will be a reckoning for them."* I didn't tell her what I thought. No, I just held her while she cried but my thoughts were simple.

I didn't think, that anyone would be made to pay, for their crimes. No, especially considering, that since Subam shutdown all News Outlets, "No one, is reporting their crimes." Shit, the only people in the News now are Subam's friends. His very own, "National News Network" and all those pricks do, is preach their Master's propaganda, in such a way, that would make Woodrow Wilson very proud.

I held Natalia for 15 minutes. Finally telling her, that I was to be transferred, before a guard came and broke us up, taking me and throwing me back in my cell. Three days later, I was transferred to the gulag. La Bastille Prison Camp in Reno Nevada. My first day here in La Bastille and all I'm getting is dirty looks, from both guards and inmates.

A guard keeps yelling at me, "Komm hur komm hur." What? I can't understand your accent. "You! Komm hur! Du blode stinkfotze!" Look, I'm sorry, I can't understand you. I'll come over. "Do sagen mien." Sir, whatever language you're speaking, I don't. "Do sagen mien." What? Aw! Shit! Ohhh! My arm! The guard I now know as "Mr. Adolfreedo Bernhard," broke my arm and raped me, for seven hours before throwing me in a cell, with some damn Russian guy.

Mr. Bernhard was hoping that the Russian would finish me off but he was cool. Even helping set my arm, using his bed sheet, to bind my arm. As he continued binding my arm, he began telling me. "My name is Victor Oleg. I was a former mercenary, working for the recently crushed resistance. I was picked up by Subam's Cheka. They took me in, under suspicion of spying, attempted assassination, and trying to form a coup. Every week, they come in here and beat me, trying to get me to sign their confession papers, so they can finally execute me." So, there's a resistance? "Not anymore!" There's not? How long have you been in here? "Two years and… *"Thinking to himself."* Six months, yes. So, tell me Pale Face… What did they pick you up on?" I attacked one of Subam's police, in an attempt to stop him, from killing a little girl.

"Really? That's not right Pale Face. This prison is for "violent criminals" against Subam's World Order. When you come here, look! The only people here, are men set to die." After dropping that bomb shell, Victor removed his shirt. His body completely covered in Russian prison tattoos. As Victor began doing push-ups, I ask, "So I suppose, this hasn't been your first time in prison?" As Victor looked up to me, he replied. "No. I grew up in Moscow.

When I was seventeen, my boyfriend and I went to a carnival, in St. Petersburg. We had a good time. I may have been young but I was in love. It was love we had enjoyed, up until a couple of fag bashers, tried roughing up my boyfriend." You're, um... gay? I asked nervously. "Yea, why? You have problem?" No, nothing like that. You just don't strike me as being gay. You just seem... Ah never mind... So, some guys were messing with your boyfriend?

"Yes, these two grisly looking fucks, were pushing him you know and pulling his hair. Now, I tried talking but they weren't listing. So, I picked up a metal pole and I rammed it through their chest's. I spent five years in "*New Kresty*." The worst years in my life before coming here..." Hey ladies, quite down! You, Indian, come with me. "Victor, what is this?" Victor sat up on his knees. "I don't know Pale, but you better go."

As I start to walk out of my cell, the guard whom took me, was a very thin black man. He grabbed my arm around the elbow. "Where are you taking me?" Just keep walking. Replied the guard. The guard walked me over to a door, while whispering. *"Once I open this door, you'll see a car."* Wait, what? *"I want you, to go to the car and get in."* As he opened the door, he pushed me through and I seen a brown cream colored car, with a woman, sticking her head out. "Pale Face, get in, now!" Natalia?

After rescuing me that night, Natalia explained the networking's, of the resistance. She would keep me safe and hidden. I spent five years in hiding. I haven't seen her after that night. She had whisked me, out and away, from certain death. Almost six years has passed, when she arrived at a safe harbor, that I've had spent most of my day's in. She needed me and after all she has done, I myself felt more than willing to help. Once again, I sat next to her and went along for the ride.

Joseph Adama

4

JAKE STALK

My quest to stop, this progressive tyranny, has failed before it even began. Now all I can do, is hope that I make it, to fight another day. Not only for my country but my son as well… As I sit here crouched behind two garbage cans, I remember a quote. *"By uniting we stand, by dividing we fall."* Yeah, those progressive pricks, they really did a good job distorting that for Collectivism.

As I crouched between two trash cans, my body "twitched," knocking one of them over. *Damn it!* I thought to myself. *Why? Why, did I twitch?* A flashlight flashes in front of my feet. I held my breath with my back against the wall. Covering my mouth, hoping to be un-heard. "There you are!" Shouted a Cheka. "We know about your plans for President Subam. Okay? So, just come out here, so that we can talk about it." Talk? *As I stood up in protest, the last thing I seen, was the flash of his side arm.*

Joseph Adama

5
HELEN'S STORY

Hello, once great people of America, my name is Helen. I came to this country, when Mr. Subam first got in. So sorry that I did. Being from European country, I know the harm from the far left, progressive people. I didn't think, this fucker Subam, would ever get in! Sad to say, I am now going to die. I wish only for my country's safety, for if Subam is anything like Hitler, he will sure enough, want to take France je t'aime France. Goodbye…

As Helen approaches her executioner, he asked her. "Do you have any last words before you go?" With tears in her eyes, she replied with a shout. "Death to Subam!" Not one-second longer after she spoke her final words, she drops and with a snap of the neck, her body dangles. The tear rolls down from her cheek and hits the floor, as if it was a splash. The room became silent.

6

DIEGO'S STORY
PART 2

Sitting in my cell I can hear men being beaten and raped. When a guard approached me, opening my cell door with a smile on his face, he begins to undo his zipper. *No! I will not be raped!* I thought to myself. I do not know what overcame me but I knocked the fucker to the floor and ran through, the open cell door. "Prisoner escaping!" Hearing, as I run through the halls. I don't even know what or where I'm running to but I constantly run as one, then two, now it seems six of Subam's fucking guards, pursuing me! *Fuck!* I thought to myself, as I approach an empty hall.

As I run through the hall, I spot an open door and beyond that, an empty room. Without giving it a second thought, I quickly ducked inside. Quietly closing the door, I look around and see a desk, along with a shit load of papers. Foreign documents and other papers that reads, *"President Subam and Guide on Foreign Policy."* As I look through the papers, I see an "Officer uniform," a size too large. I notice after further inspection, it would have to do.

After putting the uniform on, I open the door for a fast peek. Not seeing the guards, that had so very recently pursued me, or any others at the moment, I walk out. Standing in the hall, I'm able to see around allot better than before, obviously. I notice a door that reads, *"personal exit."* With a breath of joy that I've almost done, that of which I have never dreamed, "escape." I move fast for the door. As I run out, I see rows of guards.

At least twenty feet deep, with even more rows of prisoners. *God, how I feel for their poor souls.* Moving stead fast, I rushed for the gates. "Where are you heading?" Hollered one of the guards. Um, Subam's orders… I'm supposed to trace spots for landmines. Too many damn prisoners have been making it over the razor wire. "Yeah, that sounds about right." *Wow.* I thought to myself. *I can't fucking believe that worked.* Hell, I don't even know what the fuck I was talking about.

Moving quickly, I pass through the gate. *I can't believe I'm free! I'm free!* I thought to myself, as I head into the woods. Then, a thought hit me. *If a prisoner escaped, then why no lock down?*

7
CHRISTINE PAW'S STORY

Hola La gente espera mientras tu dermas Dictator Subam. I once worked in a school for autistic kids. Then Subam took control of the school and murdered, each and every one of the children. Now I live on the street sucking dick just to get by. I am so ashamed of myself, to say the least. Standing on a street corner, waiting for more men to spread my legs to, I spot Ivan. I used to be friends with him, but in a small way, he blamed me for Subam's cruel terror.

"You voted for him!" He would tell me. *"Well, that's your president! He's your, master!"* Ivan would very often, shout with anger, in his voice. To see him now, he looks so sad. *What is it he's doing on this side of town?* I wonder. *Ivan wasn't one to frequent prostitutes, unless he was dating them.* I think to myself with a smile...

"Hey Whore!" Interrupted by a man, shouting at me. "You're a cute little bitch. How much to milk this cock?" He asks me, while rubbing a bulge in his pants. Well cowboy, it depends. What are you looking for? "I want to rape that pretty fucking face of yours." I smiled at him. Yeah sexy, why don't we go back there? Looking back, I no longer see Ivan. I take this fat slob into an old abandoned factory. There was nothing sexy about this fat dirty fuck, but hey, my fucking nipples were so hard though. I was just wearing a very thin white tube-top.

I couldn't believe how erected my nipples were, after the deed was done, I didn't even have time, to wipe the jizz off my face. As nine of Subam's police officers, came busting through the door, the "dick" I was sucking, put his hands up almost immediately, as I heard one of the officers say, "Don't move Hank! What? You didn't think we would find you?" *Hmm… Is my John, some kind of resistance fighter?*

Just then, one of the police men, brought his attention over to me. "Well, look at what we found Hank." "She's just a whore." Replied Hank. "Shut it!" Shouted the other police man, in a thick, German accent. Suddenly, Hank reaches for the German officer's gun and all at once, Subam's police "shot."

Covering my face as I looked up at hank, there on the ground, his grey t-shirt turned red. Then three of the police men approached me. The first was very tall, at least 6'9 with a thin build. "Shit, you look good!" He said, with the other two just smiling, while looking down at me. I was so afraid, I just knew they were going to rape me. Out of nowhere, I felt a sharp pain on the back of my head and everything went black. When I awoken, I was in a cold, damp cell, completely naked...

8
PALE FACE
PART 2

Natalia and I didn't speak to each other for the entire drive. She pulled into a garage, that looked like a damn abandoned building. I tried asking her where we were and why she had rescued me, as we got out of the car, but she put her finger up to her pretty lips and using her soft voice, *"Just come inside. I will show you."* As she opens the door, she walks me through and I see rows, of men soldiers. Natalia then took me by my hand, whispering in my ear. *"Pale Face, we are The Resistance."* Amazing! I replied. I didn't know there really was a resistance.

Smiling, she walked me through the crowd of soldiers, telling me the beginning of their fight. "It was my late lover whose really to thank for all this. If only Carl could see now what he and Joseph started. "Joseph Adama." I don't know if you know of his work but he is one, of the few still going, that warned of Subam long, long, ago, before he was even elected. Long before Subam was even a candidate, I remember Joseph, even when Subam was nothing more than a Senator. He knew. He told me, this man was going to kill us all. Carl listened but I didn't." Natalia then frowned.

"But very few listened to him, when it could have made a difference." Just then, a soldier interrupted her. "John still hasn't returned. He went out on recon like, three fucking days ago. He should have been back by now." Did you call him? Is there no answers? "Yes, of course I called! I got nothing! I tried Sgt. Kill Joy too, still nothing! Natalia, I'm telling you, something is wrong!" Natalia then looked over to me. "Excuse me, I have to handle this." I know. I replied.

23

She introduced me to the soldier. "Pale Face, this is Richard Dead Bang Ramirez." Richard puts his hand out. "You can call me "Dead Bang." So, how long have you been in the fight? I asked. "One year… Sorry to sound sharp. I'm just worried about my friend." I understand. You're John's friend, right? "Yeah, that son of a cock sucker saved my life more than once." Looking over at Natalia, Dead Bang said, "If not for John, I'd be as dead as Carl."

Without warning, an alarm went off. "They're here!" I heard a soldier scream as Dead Bang and all the other men grabbed their guns. I looked at the surveillance cameras. As I hear Natalia gasping, "How did they find us here?" With a loud "bang," dozens of Subam's soldiers stormed the place, rushing in. With a gun in my left hand, I used the other as I grabbed Natalia, pushing her to the floor. Dead Bang was a great shot with that AR-15. He was the first to open fire and for a moment, I grinned as Subam's men fell like dominos, one right after another.

Quickly, more of the Resistance joined in. As gun fire rang out every where, I put my hand on Natalia's head. "Stay down." As I stood with only a 9 mm Glock, I began to fire, round after round. Hitting each soldier and leaving me with an empty clip. I quickly reload to a holler. "Grenade!" Then a huge explosion, left my ears ringing and bloody. The ringing in my ears, was very, frightening.

Hardly able to see much of anything, through the smoke, just seeing bodies laying everywhere. Through the smoke, I seen Subam's men picking up Natalia. I tried in vane moving towards her. I tripped over a dead body. One of the resistance soldier's, looking down, I couldn't make them out. I then seen it was Dead Bang, who lay at my feet. Looking down once more, I could see a piece of metal, sticking out of my gut.

Stupidly I started to pull it out, as more blood than I have ever seen, started running out from the wound, at a rate so fast, I thought I was dead. I thought for sure I was going to die. As I started to fall, I lost consciousness.

9
PALE FACE
PART 3

I awoke laying in a hospital bed, with tubes down my throat, as well as up my nose. A huge bandage was put across my stomach. As I tried to move, a very tall man approached me. He wasn't a doctor. "You have been out for quite some time. Yes, many months. "Don't move too much." As he spoke, he reached for something, it's another tube. He moved closely, with his left hand and began shoving the tube, down my throat.

I lay here gagging, while the tube is being shoved down my throat. Looking up in pure terror, I look at this man, without a clue as to what day, let alone the month it is. The man continues speaking. "You and your little girlfriend are lucky. You may not think so, considering your current situation. The two of you, were the only ones that survived the raid, on your little party." Wickedly smirking, he continues. "Well, you almost didn't but one thing I know Redskin, your story is impressive. You have some luck, you know, considering all in all." Interrupting his statement, a nurse wearing a very short skirt walks in, over to where I lay. She puts her hand on my neck and at that moment, a pinch. As a needle goes in my neck, I begin to slowly, rest my eyes.

10
CHRISTINE PAW'S STORY
PART 2

The cell I found myself laying in, was very cold and damp. As I stood up, I covered my breasts, with my left arm. Looking around, I couldn't see any, other soul. For hours, I stood naked, alone and cold in this cell. Three hours passed, when a guard approached. *What does he want?* I wondered. "Hello, Cherie." Why am I naked?

"Now calm down. I'll be the one asking questions! Now, why were you with that man?" I'm a prostitute. "All right Cherie. Did you know who that man was?" No! "Dis moi la verite! Cherie…" What? Please, I don't understand... "Mais non Cher. I'm sorry sweetie. Now, just don't lie and everything will be fine." Okay, yes Sir. I will be cooperative. I didn't know that man. I was standing on the street "hooking," when he approached me saying, he wanted his cock sucked. So I took him into that old factory, to suck on his dick, that's all.

"Okay Cherie. Now, do you want to get down?" What? You want me to suck your dick? With a smile. "Oh Cherie, I'm asking if you want out of your cell." You're going to let me go? "Well Cherie, they may not like it but I think dem boys are wrong about you. So I tell you what Cherie, I've had nuff! Subam, he just not right… Mo chagren Cherie, I never meant to scare you."

What is your name? "Luke." He replied. My new friend Luke, walked down the hall, to check for other guards. "I think it's clear." Luke whispers as he's walking back. "I think it's clear Cherie." Luke opened the door of my cell. I look down, still completely naked. "I can't walk out like this!" No Cherie, even as beautiful as you are, just walk out with me. I'll get you something to cover yourself. As we walked out, he turned to me, looking down at my naked body, telling to me, "je te'desire."

Luke, then walked me over to a hamper, that sat at the door, near the guard's station. Reaching in behind the door, he pulls out a very large t-shirt and small children's sized pair of shorts. "I got these for you, ma Cherie." I stare at the shorts saying, I will never fit them. Just, give me the shirt. "All right, Cherie."

11

PALE FACE
THE CONCLUSION

When I awoke, I was no longer in a hospital bed. Instead, I was Strapped down to a cold metal table. Wanting to call out, I realized my mouth was sewn shut. *"God No!"* I yelled to myself. I heard a voice. Someone was speaking but I couldn't see anyone! "Danke, mein freund. Schon dich kennen zu lernen. I have heard many great things of you, mein freund. You and I are going to have allot of fun together. Sorry about your mouth but I'm not someone who likes screaming."

As the door opened, I seen this man, walk through. "Hi mein freund!" He must have been, at least 6'4 dressed in all black. He walked over to me, laying on the cold metal table. "Wow, you are a sight." He told me, while adjusting the table. I was no longer on my back but now, sitting up right. This man towered over my 5'6-inch frame. "Now, lets see what we can do." The sick son of a bitch said. He reminded me of a Nazi, from an old war movie. There was a table next to him. He picked up many long pins. As he smiled, this evil man didn't waste time, sticking the long needles, inside my body.

Removing the bandage across my stomach, he began slowly, inserting the needles. My God, how I wanted to scream. He took a needle, removing a pair of boxers I had been wearing. He pushed the needle, into my Penis, as if it was a "catheter." The needle bent, poking through the top of my Penis. As I sat in pain, I felt two more needles! One going into my face, right under my left eye, as the other was slowly pushed into my throat. "Ich bin Der meinung, this look suits you Indian." He then lifted his left hand, striking me across my face, before walking out. leaving me strapped down, with pins, still stuck in

29

my body...

Hours later, a woman entered the room. She was not, the same woman I had encountered earlier. "Hello there, Savage! I'm sorry about Albert. He can get, a little carried away." *"This bitch is anything but "sorry."* I thought to myself. Walking over, she continued talking. "Oh, you poor baby." As she stroked my face, she smiled. "You won't be using, "that" again." Pointing down towards my exposed penis, ripped and bleeding. She then took a knife and began "skinning" my penis. "I'm going too have fun with you. Maybe, more than that bitch, you came here with." She then began kissing me. First my neck, she then slowly worked her way down, stopping when she reached my destroyed penis. I then felt a "tug." *My Penis!* She held it up for me to see.

With terror in my eyes, I could feel myself start to bleed out. "Now." She said. "I will let you speak. If you still value your life, you will tell me everything, I want to hear." She cut the stitching, freeing my mouth. As I coughed up blood, I wanted to scream at her! I wanted her dead! I wanted to kill this bitch! I could feel myself passing out. She shouted. "No, wake up! You will talk! Tell me, what you know of the resistance! I promise, I will end your pain savage!" She said. You're going to die. Now, we can make it quick or I can continue to drag out your suffering. So talk! Tell me, what you know of this resistance! Just then, an alarm went off. "Shit!" She said. Two soldiers, entered the room.

"What the Hell is happening?" She desperately asked the men. Ma'am, we're on lock down. "What? One of you fucks, tell me, what's happening!" Ma'am, the base is under attack! Several resistance fighters have infiltrated the base! Just as the frightened soldier finished speaking, I heard shots being fired. Ma'am! We must get you to a secure location! "No, you fool!" She replied. "The prisoner!" She cried, pointing at me.

I could feel myself dying, as the soldier said. "Fuck him! He's dead already!" Come on, ma'am, we need to get you out of here! "No! Not without finishing him! Give me your side arm!" The balding soldier who had remained quite, the entire time watching the door, removed his piece. She then took it without hesitation. She fired two shots into my chest. The last thing I seen, was the light flickering, on the wall, as I could hear, "the battle cries of war."

It all went black.

Joseph Adama

CHAPTER 12

My name is Salvictor Marceau. Moments ago, my men and I stormed "Subam's military base." Damn me for not acting sooner. Subam's thugs raided one of our havens four months ago. Only recently had it been confirmed by my people that our top commander was being held here. As soon as I gave the green light, my men and I wasted no more time. I quickly, took action.

"Sargent!" I could hear one of my men calling out to me. As I looked back I see my comrade "Saturday. Jimmy Saturday," yelled at me. "Sargent, help!" He had a huge hole in his chest. *I wish I could have comforted my fallen brother.* I quickly came back to reality. *I'll make Saturday's death, mean something!* As I keep moving, I hear Private "Hard Bay" panting, as we climb over body's of our fallen comrades, as well as enemies alike. "So much death..." Hard Bay commented.

As my men and I rushed through the doors, blowing them open, two Doctor's jumped out at us with guns in hand. Hard Bay put them both down before they could fire a shot. "Keep moving!" I shouted. As we continued inside, the building seemed empty. As we moved room by room, I yell to my men or what's left of them, to spread out. Signaling for Hard Bay to move towards the left side of the hall, as private Starkweather took position, he pulled out the pin from his grenade.

As I was going to give the signal, shots rang out. "I'm hit!" Hard Bay yelled. "Sit rep!" I ordered. "Sit rep, sir! We're under fucking attack!" Starkweather shouted, "We need to find where the shots are being directed from. We need to return fire! Sir, Sargent! Sgt. Marceau!" Starkweather frantically shouted as I just stood there in a daze. "Oh, my dick…"

The expression I heard from Starkweather. "Marceau has been hit!" With that, I looked down, almost as if in slow motion, my body went limp. "Shit, Salvictor's dead! Keep clear of the windows and keep moving! "Fuck!" Stay low!"

13
VIVI LA REVOLUTION

I'm Jerry Dead Fox McCoy. As I'm reporting to you now, I can see we're fucked. Only moments ago, Sgt. Marceau ordered the assault on Subam's compound. We now appear to be barricaded in. Damn it! Salvictor's dead! No one here is going to be alive when the smoke clears. I'm pined down in a dark room. There's a dead man. His body strapped down. Needles sticking from his body. This poor bastard was tortured. His mouth, savagely sewed closed.

I only hope, Natalia did not suffer such a fate, as I know what few of us remain, will not be able to reach her. As reality sets in, I know, she's probably just as dead. I thought to myself...

14

AND THE SMOOTH TOUNGE ROLLED OUT

Last night, rebels attacked a marine hospital, igniting a fire fight. Our glorious leader Subam was quick to act, extinguishing the threat. President Subam's police force was engaged, for four hours with the terrorist rebels, before our brilliant wonderful leader Subam, ordered for bombs to be dropped on the area. Thus, extinguishing those threats.

15

THE SORROWFUL CHEKA

I laugh in disgust as I hear the news report. My name's Joseph Birdman and I was there. I'm not proud of the fact that I'm one of President Subam's "Cheka." A job I have grown more ashamed of as time goes. I first joined for the same reasons, as many others, I believed in James Subam. I believed in his "vision." What he was doing wasn't for us. It was for the great, majority of our people.

How foolish could I have been. I look around my house and see metals of various types. Metals I received from raping, killing and setting fire to people's home's, while they slept. I remember watching a woman screaming and pleading, as I poured gasoline all over, her two children. I made her watch as they screamed, crying out as they burnt to death. I'm no hero. I'm nothing more than a murderer.

I remember my Ex-girlfriend. I didn't want her to have part in my life, for her safety. I kept her out, never was I able to tell her the truth. I cried aloud, reading her last email to me. I made her hate me, only to keep her alive. But I'm not a man. I'm only an extinction of the great Subam. So when orders came down, she was named an enemy of our beloved state, so I killed her.

My phone lights up. It's a call, from my commander. Hello sir. *"Yes, Mr. Birdman? Your wanted at area 16-A."* After informing me that I was needed, he hung up. Well, here I go. Off to lick the feet of my master. As I go out to my car, some neighbor kids salute me. "Hail Subam!" I return the salute. "Siege Heil!" What a fraud I am... Cowards in fancy uniforms. I'm no soldier.

Getting into my car, I turn on the radio. Big mistake... Every station I turned to, it's all propaganda, "Subam's Mouth Piece." *"I've been on the road for 20 minutes, passing a work camp."* These fucking people, live in filth! What use to be free citizens, are now permanently imprisoned, for nothing more, than resisting slavery. Starving and broken down, they're rotting. Fucking fools, nothing more now than "surf's." After 40 minutes, I've arrived at area 16-A.

Fucking place is empty. Stepping out from my car, I see my commanding officer approach. "Greetings Joseph, you made great time." Yes sir, Mr. Burrows... "Don't move Birdman, snipers." *"My entire body is covered in red dots. I'm brought here to die. I'm nothing more than cattle and them, they're the damn ranchers."* "Tell me Mr. Birdman, should we kill you?" I'm a loyal servant of our glorious Subam.

As I proclaim my love for Subam. A very thin bald man, interrupted me. Is that all, Mr. Birdman? You do understand, that your life is in danger. Why sir? Joseph Birdman, your life is very much, at risk here... You have no idea, why we would question your loyalty? Joseph, think about the friends you keep. What friends, sir? I will refresh your memory.

Does Joseph Adama, mean anything to you? That is right Mr. Birdman, we know, of your relationship with Joseph Adama. He is resistance Mr. Birdman, but you knew that. Sir, I'm a loyal Socialist. I'm proud, to serve our Great Leader! Hail Subam! I don't want to die. I serve the Socialist order. Why and how could a proud Socialist, a member of the great Cheka, have any relation, to an Anti-Communist Propagandist, like Adama? The pure filth alone, he writes "All men are free and equal." Sir, what do you need me to do? Prove your loyalty, not only to President Subam but to all Communists! Kill, Joseph Adama." Yes sir, I will do as you wish.

16

JOSEPH BIRDMAN
TO KILL A HERO TO SAVE A COWARD

Hours after I leave, I feel the shuttering decision, sinking in. I can murder the last real voice of the people and in doing so, murder the last true hope, for the American people. There shall be no hope for a free America, for if I warn Adama, I then seal my fate, damning myself. Warning Adama is certain death. Am I really that big of a coward? That I would murder a hero? A brave man speaking out against evil? In doing so, I would damn a nation. For what? Only to save my own skin?

I was told when, as well as where, to meet with Adama. He would be speaking at an underground, Anti-Communist Rally. I will shoot him, as he begins to speak. I'll do as I'm told. What's one more life? Adama really believes, I'm a man on the inside, who he can trust. If only he could see, the monsters he preached against, when they, where right in front of him. Adama, much like my late girlfriend Kara, won't see it coming. In my own personal way, I would like to say, "Goodbye." I have played both sides of the fence. At times, giving their resistance, side notes and tips.

I call Adama before I arrive at his rally, an hour before he is set to give his speech. Greetings Adama, it's Birdman. *"Is something wrong?"* No, I just wanted to say Goodbye. Just know that, your fight has meaning. *"Why are you saying this Birdman?"* I must go. Hanging up the phone, I waited for Adama to take the stage. Ten minutes into Adama's speech, I shot him twice in the head, with a .45 caliber. A hero was dead, as with him, what hopes America had for liberty, has died. With him, any hopes for freedom, are now lost.

Sitting at home, around the safety of a job well done, I'll be receiving a congratulation call. I think to myself, watching the news broadcast, about Adama's Death… *"An enemy of our great state, has been shot by one of his own followers. It has been reported, that there had been discontent in their ranks."* Turning off the TV. "Bullshit!" I think to myself. *Subam's news reporters did a good job on this one.* Turning the TV back on, almost for kicks. Hell, they had a fucking innocent man, some 23-year-old, the news reporter just ID as Sam Tucker and now, he's going to be put to death for my crime. Someone's calling, probably to thank me for a job well done?

Hello? *"Hey, Mr. Birdman, good job. I just seen the news… You'll be getting a big reward, for this one. Now, Mr. Birdman, I know, I know, that the other guys didn't think you had it in you but I knew, you could do it Birdman. I'm sorry if we put you in a difficult situation. You know, I wouldn't have let harm come to you. You're the tip of the spear Joseph! Thank you."*

Thank you, Rob. I'm proud to have served Subam. Heil Subam! *"So, tell me Joseph, how did it feel?"* Come on Robert, you killed before. *"Yeah, I know, but you killed Joseph Adama. Come on now, you know that means something, to the guys upstairs. He was a head figure in the propaganda machine."* Robert, I know what you're saying and I know, you wouldn't have allowed me to be shot, you're right. I just don't want to talk now. *"All right, Joseph. Hero, you have a good night. Get laid or something. My cousin's love for Subam, is unreal!"* Robert really believes in what he's doing but he's right, I could use some pussy. I'm calling a prostitute.

17

BIRDMAN'S STORY
WHAT IS GOING ON

After I paid this whore for a job well done, I decide to get some rest, with my cock still wet, with her smell. I'm too exhausted to shower now. I'm gonna sleep in for a while and I'll make sure, to set my alarm. I wake up to see it's after 12:00 P.M. *"Shit."* I thought to myself. I overslept! The one thing, you can't do, in the line of work I'm in! Looking at my phone, I see that I've missed 14 calls and nine text messages. I check the voicemail, finding out it's my superior officer. All but two, of the text messages, were from him. As for the other two, non related messages I had, were sent from a British prostitute I fuck, once in a while.

She's super natural and so tight. I think to myself, for a brief moment. Her message reads, *"Hey Joe, I'm wet. Come over baby."* The second is a *"Heart Icon,"* with the words, *"Fuck Me."* Ignoring her text, I immediately get dressed. According to my superior's message, we have a problem. He last called me, at 10:00 A.M. No telling what the situation is at this point. I quickly turn on the TV, to see there's nothing being reported.

No mention of trouble. Of course I can't go by that, with no "Freedom of Press." *I hear something in my house.* "Anyone there?" I shout, while picking up a .38 special. I see a shadow and I "shoot." I see a man, move out from my hallway. Quickly he flees, as I pursue him into the living room. I look around, when I feel a sharp pain in my neck. Everything, goes black...

I wake up to see it is dark outside. I rose to my feet, looking around, I could see my house was trashed. My metals, destroyed. "Who did this?" Thinking aloud. As for that matter, what were they looking for? I notice my cellphone was broken on the floor. I have to get to sub level 9. It's 7:38 P.M. when I notice the emergency broadcast came on.

Flipping through channels, I see the EBS is on every station. *"This broadcast, is warning people to stay indoors."* The voice on the broadcast keeps repeating. *"Don't provoke the craft. Officers, don't fire at the craft. The craft is unknown. Your beloved leader Subam, warns that it may be potentially, dangerous."* What craft?

I take a moment to think, what is going on. I look around for my side arm or even the .38 special I was holding, before hitting the floor. Unarmed, I walk outside. I freeze in disbelief, for what I am witnessing, is not possible. Aloud I think to myself, *"this can't be happening."* Terror swept my face. Fear, has set in. I can't move.

18

AND THE WHORE CAME FORTH

Sporting the XXL red shirt, Luke had lead me to safety. Hey, Cherie, Dem boys not be smart. I told you, I could get you out. Dem boys, not even know your pretty body is missing. Not till, it's too late anyway. Luke, where are we going? Shh... Cherie, just stay close to me. I continued following Luke, through the different halls. We passed some guards and with Luke, being the smart man that he is, told them I was commander Damien's "Sex Toy."

Luke, will that really work? Relax Cherie, dem boys won't dare, question Damien. Dat boy is running dis here "Sha-Bang!" Hey, Cherie, right there, we go. Luke, pointed to a door as he spoke. Dats our way out, Cherie. *Could it really be this easy?* I thought to myself. Luke walked me over to the door. Go Cherie. Go? Wait, what about you? Maybe Cherie, 'ñe ťen fais pas pour moi je vais bien, dem boys won't do bad to me now. You want to get down on this place? Go Cher! Just like that, I left him.

In my mind, I seen myself kiss him but I just ran. I ran deep into the woods and I didn't stop running. Even as the shirt I had been wearing, became ripped. God, I felt like I was running for hours...

Joseph Adama

19

THEY CAME IN FORCE BIRDMAN

The sky appears black, "Pitch Black," save for a metallic shine. I could barely make out at first, coming back from my stillness, I look out in the street. It seemed empty. I start to walk forward from my porch, into the street. I could see lights from the ground. They were far off in the distance but it was definitely, military. I don't know how far off they are, maybe 20 "clicks."

Shit. Thinking to myself, as I looked up at the sky, *I wonder if my car even works*. Crossing my fingers, I get into my car as I put the key in the ignition and to my surprise, started right up. I drove through the streets, with myself being the only car on the deserted road, the streets remained empty. As I approached the military blockade, two Privates rushed to my vehicle, with their XM25 rifles.

"Sir? Sir, get out of the car. This is a restricted area." As I stepped out, making sure that my hands were in their sight, one of the men grabbed me, pushing me to the floor. Even with their gun's drawn on me, I knew once they learned who I was, I would be briefed by their Superior and learn what was going on here. As one of the soldiers began searching my car, a bright light shot out from the distance.

20
DANEIL DAVIS'S STORY

I've been on death row since June 14, 1985, at San Quentin Prison. It's December 22, 2020. I was 21 years old, when I was first sentenced, here to San Quentin. Do the math, never mind the fact that I'm completely innocent… I was arrested, charged, and later, convinced of the murders of eight women. Being branded a fucking serial killer.

You can never imagine the disgust, as well as anger, I've felt then and still feel to this day. My whole life is gone. I'm 56 years old, my mother came to this country from Scotland and my father from Russia. As a child, they would always tell me how lucky I was, to be born in America. My family was very proud, to call themselves Americans. Not once, did either one, lose hope in the country nor the system.

Up until their death, they believed my conviction would be overturned and I would be set free. In the words of my mother, *"This is the land of the free. If you did nothing wrong, then they must see that and let you go."* My mother was always the optimist. Prison got a lot worse when that Socialist Democratic, son of a bitch, took power. First Subam ordered all prisoners, to be used for slave labor. Those of us on death row, were used as genie pigs. Those of us still able to move around, were denied all forms of comfort, to the point that we're just sitting in empty cells, sleeping on cold cement floors.

Today is announced as my execution, the 22nd of December. *Well, mom* "I think to myself." *Perhaps if a socialist, hadn't taken your land of the free, I would have a chance. We all would but no, we now live in the United Socialist States of Subam!*

I've spent my life in this cell. I've lived longer in prison than I lived as a free man. Death is the only real freedom, we have left. Shit, I can't wait to die. Put an end to this madness.

It was Lenin who coined, *"the youth useful idiots."* When Mr. Subam first ran, it was teens, some not even old enough to vote, that marched in the streets. Watching T.V in my cell, I saw a reporter ask the teens, why they were protesting. Most had no clue they were marching for Subam. Yet, most did not know, his first name or what he stood for.

Well, they wanted their wonderful peaceful utopia, their Communist promise land. I sometimes wonder what those fucking kids, those pot smoking, Mao loving, Che Guevara wannabes, think of their peaceful James Subam. After all, that he has done, I wonder how many still love him?

I remember a Pen Pal I once had. He began writing me in January of 2010. We had corresponded over a hundred times from 2010 to 2020. He was not a fan of Subam and for that reason, I believe he was murdered. He stopped writing me. I know he would never have done that, if he was still alive. Siting here, I remember the words of President Reagan, *"There are no constraints on the human mind. No walls around the human spirit. No barriers to our progress except those we ourselves erect."* And the day America elected Subam, we did just that. As I sit here, on the cold floor, I wonder if this land my mother once loved, will ever be free once more.

21
THE MAT SAID "WELCOME"
CHRISTINE'S FINAL

Finally, after miles of running, I just collapsed. My knees cut. My body is so weak, with exhaustion. In my mind, I had thought, I was running forever. Forever, turned out only being one or two hours. I laid almost completely naked. The XXL red shirt no longer covering my body, I use it to wrap my waist, when some guy and his girlfriend found me. Not sure if I could trust them, I lied when asked, "Hey honey, are you all right?"

Oh, um yeah. I replied. I guess, I just had a fight with my boyfriend. "Did he beat you up?" The girl asked, looking down at my body. Yes. I replied. Well, do you have anywhere to stay? Um... No, I don't Well, what's your name? I'm Christine. The man came forward. "I'm Rave, this is my gal, Molly." Molly stepped forward. "Hi." I just smiled and waved, trying to keep my breast covered.

The couple took me back to their place, a little apartment. After getting cleaned up, I sat in a cozy little rocking chair. Molly brought me something to eat. Thank you for your help. Molly smiled replying, "It's OK." After eating the two very delicious hamburgers on my plate, I felt very tiered. I asked, where I could sleep. Rave took me into a room, where I could sleep. I thanked him as he put his hand on my waist. As I was only wearing a towel, he said in a soft voice, "There's some clothes on the dresser." Rave then turned and walked out. Two minutes later, I fell asleep.

The next morning, I awoke to Rave, sitting at the end of my bed. He handed me a glass of orange juice. "Thank you." I noticed in his lap, he had a piece of paper. What's that? I asked. Rave just got up and left the room. Wearing the panties and t-shirt molly had given me, I got up and walked into the kitchen, where I seen Molly. "Good morning." Said Molly, as I just smiled her way.

When I was going to speak, I heard a phone ring. Rave quickly came into the kitchen, grabbing the cell off the counter. *"Must be something important."* I thought, as I shrugged to myself. "So, how do you feel, this morning?" Asked Molly. Um, I'm okay. *"Considering, I wanted to ask, about Rave but I just held my tongue."* So Christine, are you hungry? Oh um... Looking over at the toaster, I replied, a piece of toast would be fine. Oh Honey, I'll do you better than a piece of toast. Sit down, I'll make you some eggs.

After I ate, Molly gave me some of her sister's clothes. After putting them on for the first time, I had something that fit, since this ordeal. Thinking as I was smiling to myself, *"Somebody actually gave me clothes, that fit my body perfect."* After getting dressed, I walked into the living room. "Looking good," said Rave. I replied, "Thanks!" With a smile. Rave and I sat in silence for almost five minutes.

That's when he turned to me saying, "Those clothes fit you well." Yep I replied. Rave then stood up and came over to me. As I sat looking up at him, he put his hands on my face, moving in to kiss me. I put my arms around his waist. He was pulling at my tight, fitting, shirt from Molly's sister. Rave pushed me back onto the Sofa, kissing me hard. Just as molly walked in...

22
IVAN VALENTIN'S STORY
PART 1

It's funny me being here. I always thought, I would go out in style in a "Blaze of Glory." Shooting it out with the enemy like "Rambo." Not sitting in a "cell" waiting to die, with other condemned men. No, I got sloppy. I was tired of the so called "Patriots." They talked about resisting and fighting back against "Subam's brutal tyranny." I knew Subam's presidency, would be the "ultimate death," of America.

I think back to myself, sitting on the couch with Joseph, watching *"The Exodus of Thousands of Americans"* on TV. *"Many Americans fled to Canada, even more, into Mexico."* Joseph and I sat there watching. Sadness came over the both of us. Ivan, we should try to get out of here too. No. I replied. I won't leave my "country." "Then, what do we do?" We fight. You're right in theory Ivan, the only problem is, that these Communist's loving coward's, are stupid and Subam's supporters out number us greatly, so if we're going to fight, we need support. Americans are stupid. They don't know or care about the "history" or anything else. Just a bunch of idiots, giving up "freedom" for free stuff, as they throw out their freedoms, in exchange for "safety." I'm going to write pamphlets. I'm going to try, to wake these idiots up." Hey Joey, I'm going to head out.

It's funny, "I thought to myself." *Joey's idea. He thinks that he can wake these idiots up, with "pamphlets?"* Right... "I think to myself." *I'm disgusted, as I see the street. Fucking fools, celebrating their "beloved Communists Victory."* Yeah, "I thought to myself." *We'll see how happy you are, when your food is taken away and later "Rationed." Yeah, taken away, along with all your "freedom's."*

When I arrived at my "friend's house," I found him just sitting there, on his couch outside. You look relaxed. "Hey Ivan, how the hell are you?" How am I? Jake, are you serious? Of course, I'm being serious. Jake, I've known you for what? Seven years? "SÍ amigo." Now, a fucking "Communist," has just taken over "my, country!" Jake, how do you think I am? Wow, Ivan come on man. What Jake, are you fucking kidding me? A Communist, just became "President," of the United States. What's wrong with you? Jake, seriously man. Are you fucking blind? Jake, don't you understand what this means?

We both, thought Hannity was bad. He was a fucking "moderate," compared to fucking, Subam. Jake, wakeup! We're all going to die! We'll be killed! Ivan we're not going to be killed. I honestly think you're being dramatic. You always think, it's going to be worse, than it is. Sit down and have a beer. No! I'm not going, to sit down and act, like nothing's wrong! You're fucking nuts! Ivan, where you going? I don't know but I'll tell you one thing, if necessary, I'm going to war. War for my country. War against tyranny. Aren't you talking treason? Sometimes, the traitor turns out being the most patriotic, one of them all…

After leaving Jake's house, I couldn't stop thinking about how damn foolish and in the dark, he is. After about ten minutes of walking, I passed a store and decided to stop and go in, for a little shopping. After grabbing a few things, I stood in line listing to two people, talk about "How wonderful, the new leader was." After those clowns left, it was my turn. After buying two loafs of bread, a candy bar, as well as some smokes, the clerk said, "Hail Subam!" I just turned and walked out.

Returning home, I seen Joseph siting on the porch, smoking a cigarette. Hey bro! "Wassup!" Looking up, he replied, "Wuzz up!" Just a way we have always come to greet each other. "So, what you been up to?" Joseph asked. Shit man, Jake's nuts. Joseph smirked saying, "Look around man, everyone is." Yeah, so you still think that writing pamphlets will wake the country up?

It's not. You know these useful idiots won't listen. I know Ivan, you're right but "One man with a gun can control a hundred men without." "Just as one man's idea, can wake up 100 that are sleeping." So yeah, the name Joseph Adama, will be a name known for awareness, justice, and freedom."

No Joey, it won't work. This Communist "bitch" Subam, won't allow it. Look man, I'm serious. I'm fighting. I can't force you to join me but I can't do it without you bro. I'm with you man, no doubt, I'm in but we seriously, need time. We need to build a resistance. Find like minded people, who are willing to fight, for the freedom's, we so desperately forgot we had. Ivan, if I can distribute "pamphlets," we can get followers. Joey seriously, like anyone will even look, at your "pamphlets."

Look around. There's men, "marching in boots." I see "children, pledging allegiance to Subam." Our entire country changed. This is not, America and I don't know if it ever will be again. I will die, before I kneel. You seen the news? "Yeah, Canada's prime minister just signed his "oath" to Subam. He said Canada welcomed Subam." Yeah, he did. So much for fleeing... "Fuck, Canada is five minutes from becoming a "fascist state." No, Joey, Canada will be Subam's State. "All right man, I'm out."

After Joseph left, I thought about what he had said. *"Fucking Canada, their prime minister, The S.O.B is going to run his country like "Mussolini." As for Mexico. Fuck Mexico! Ten years ago it was drug cartels and now it's "radical Islamist," that owns that fucking country."*

Joseph Adama

23
IVAN VALENTIN'S STORY
PART 2

The next day, I got ready for war. I got ready, to die. As I watched myself in the mirror, I was prepared for death. I was almost expecting it. Without help, I had no chance. I knew what I was doing, could be called suicide. A man I met, named "Carl," he said he could help. He said, that he would help me, to bring war against that son of a whore, Subam.

He was a "Military Man," who knew just how to bring down, a tyrant. Not only to plan and execute the attack but how, we could get away with it as well. Carl told me, "We're not going to die. We can win. We can takedown, this "Democratic Socialist Regime!" We can and will win a fight, that we are heavily, outnumbered in." I went with Carl. His plan was simple, "Rise up, take our fight to the top." Carl made plans, as I grew more and more ready, to fight. I decided, Carl wasn't serious or at least, not as much as I felt I was.

I spotted some blind spots, around the police station. While walking pass, *"Yeah,"* I thought to myself, *"That's where I'll strike."* Later that night, I returned with pipe bombs. Planting them to the rear side of the "entrance," to the "police station." After planting the bombs, I quickly made my escape, back into the street, not thinking about the security cams. *"What I do, I do for liberty."* I thought, as I flea to safety.

That morning, the police station, went up in a "boom." I've began my life as a "Gorilla Fighter." I found myself, upon a T.V station that was playing, *"Breaking News."* When without warning, my "face showed up on the screen." Watching in horror, my phone rang. *"Ivan, fuck man, this is Joseph. You gotta move. You're all over the TV. What the "fuck," did you do?"* My face was on every station. *"The suspect's name is Ivan Valentin, he's 5'8 inches tall and 170 lbs. He has brown hair as well as multiple tattoos, including a skull, on his left forearm."* "Shit! Ivan, seriously. Get out man. You got the *"whole city, looking" for you!"* Just as Joseph said that, I dropped my phone.

There's men at my front door. I quickly jump out my window. As I made my exit, I heard my door being kicked in. I see police on the street. *"Oh shit!"* Jumping a fence, leading into the alley, *I can easily lose them.* I thought, *in one of the side streets.* Well, until I seen the helicopter, over my head. *"Shit."* Then, I got an idea. Running through a series of back streets, I remembered a "manhole," at the very end of one of the neighborhoods, right before the freeway. Without hesitation, I jumped down into the manhole, hitting the bottom hard. Screaming in pain, with the sound of a "snap!" I knew, I broke my leg. Sure, it was a desperate move but these are the times of desperation.

24
ANGEL GAMUETA'S
STORY PART 1

"Hey Angel, Get in here!" Yes, sir. What do you need? "Pick all this shit, up in my room." Yes, sir… After your done with that, crawl over here and "blow me." Life in China was hard enough. Adding on top of that, being a "sex slave" each and everyday, I was made to serve scores and scores of strange men. Long have I dreamed of America. "The land of Liberty" and "Life, of true freedom." Little did I know but I would soon get that chance.

As an "American man" walked into my shop, he requested a blow job. Eagerly, I stood with a "smile," hoping to be chosen. Standing there, I played back speeches, from the "American presidents," I had memorized. *"Ask not what your country can do for you but what you can do for your country."* Thinking back to John Kennedy's word's I thought to myself, *"I will do anything, for your country."* Just then, my boss walked over to me saying, "Yes Mr. Subam. "She's tight." You want her?" Pointing to me, my face lit up.

25

JOSEPH BIRDMAN'S STORY PART 5
AND THE WORLD CHANGED AGAIN

The light was hot and blinding. I could hear "screaming," from all around me, yet for reasons of "fear," combined with that blinding light, I had just laid there, still "frozen" as if I were a "stone," with my "face," in the dirt for 20 minutes, before "mustering" up the courage, to stand. As I did, I seen that my car, along with all military vehicles, were now gone. I stood there "alone." With not a "soul" in sight. It was as if, I was standing, in a ghost town. Looking up at the object, I see it sitting, "calmly" in the Sky. *What the "fuck," is going on?* I ask myself. Then suddenly, out of nowhere, I'm grabbed by two men, taking me away. What's happening? I ask. They reply, "Shut up and keep moving." After they took me into some sort of "underground bunker," I ask again. What the fuck, is going on? One of the men opened his "mouth," as he began speaking, I stood "quite".

"As of now, it would appear, that we're at war with... "Outside forces." Some sort of "unknown, beings" that of which..." Interrupting him, almost at a complete loss." This can't be possible. Are we talking "Aliens?" How is this possible? "Three weeks ago, we received a signal. President Subam felt, it is best to..." What? I ask. Keep it quiet? You knew! Yet, nothing was done? Joseph, shut up and listen.

We don't know much, about these things but our "beloved Communist Empire," has allot more to "fear," than these creatures. We needed to keep our attention on those who, threatened our great Subam. We felt, it was our main priority. What? You knew, that this was coming, yet you wasted time, executing small groups of rebels? As the man, looked to the ground he said,

"What we know, about these "things," they don't bleed, if they feel fear or pain, they don't show it.

Mr. Birdman, half of our country is gone. What? "Yeah," the second man spoke. "These things wiped out the entire, east coast and most of Canada is "gone." O.K. *taking a breath* I ask, So, what's our plan? "Our great leader Subam, will lead our people, out of this great crisis. As for you, Mr. Birdman, where do you stand?" With the human race! "And your thought's, on our Great Leader's plans?" I look to these psychotic men, obviously delusional, in their "love for Subam." I reply, I stand with you. I stand, with our Great Leader Subam.

Out of nowhere, my face was splashed with blood. I heard taping as the man standing in front of me, fell to the floor. Standing there, over his body, was a small silver creature with three legs. It had spikes moving out from its arm's. The second man fired his gun, as one creature, became many. He shot "frantically," hitting me in my side. Looking down, I see one of them is almost inspecting me.

26

DAN'S STORY
THE DEVILS IN THE DETAILS

"I awake to death Battered bodies and rotting flesh. Scratch marks cover my chest. Women's pleas and empty screams. Caged whores locked behind doors. As I stand covered in blood knife in hand, my mat always says welcome."

I went on a hunt last night. Subam's police force can make it hard at times but not this night, no. I caught myself a prize. A sweet young, looking "little bitch." I've seen her walking with two other girls. Waiting for them to separate, I watched her, as I masturbated. Then I seen my chance. I pulled my van up beside her.

Hey sweetie, can I give you a ride? The bitch just kept walking. Come on "honey," it's getting "dark out." Let me give a lift. "No thank you, sir. I'm fine." *Fuck this little bitch.* I thought to myself. Jumping out of my van, I grabbed her. She screamed and started biting me. Thinking fast, I brought out my "knife." Yeah, that silenced the bitch, real nice. Forcing her into my van, I made sure she buckled in for safety. Suddenly, a "bright blue light," filled the night sky. "What the fuck!" I said aloud.

27
LISA'S STORY
THE PROPHET'S GIRLFRIEND

I never paid attention to politics nor much anything else. As a little girl, I dreamed of becoming a model. "So pretty, she is." My mom would always hear from anyone, who seen me but coming to age, in this lost time, inside a world without hope, seeing my mother die at the hands of Subam's police force, the very same day my boyfriend, the "Thomas pain of our generation," was shot dead. I can't believe one of his supporters, would do such a thing, but if they got Joseph and my mom, they'll get me. So, I do as Joseph once said, "I choose my own fate." With that thought, I take my last breath.

28
JOSEPH ADAMA'S STORY
THE PROPHET'S LAST WORDS

This world makes me sick. I knew what Subam was. I read the "quatrains of Nosterdamus." No one listened. No one cared, until it was too late but these people, these "useful idiots!" They did this! They voted for this world, we're all now trapped in. The American people chose safety, over "freedom," for bad and worse. I don't care at this point. I just hope the horrible "undoing," will soon come forth.

I've been on the front lines as a one-man news source. The only person "actually" acknowledging or able to get the message out, to "acknowledge," that not everyone is happy, here in Subam's "utopia," of democratic order. It's 8:23 A.M. Shit, I've been living nomad so long. I'm starting to forget, what it was like to have a place to hang my hat.

I write pamphlets, news articles, things like that. I try to do my best, so those who won't kneel, can see they're not alone. I also try to point out, that this "new world order" of "social justice," is not only in the hands of Subam but any of those, whom voted for him. Whether or not you've come to regret it, this new world is the direct fault, of the "American people" and the lack of their understanding, about what "America" was meant to be! Our country, was once a land built on three principles of law. A rule that "All men were created equal." Yet, now look at what you lack, caring and plain stupidity, has brought us to a point of pure madness!

After I wash up, I get ready by going through my notes. I give Nika a call. *"She's got eye's, everywhere it seems."* Hello? *"Hi, Yuseph."* Hey, so how are things looking with the birds? *"No birds, today... It has been raining."* Really,

Nika? Well, time to put your "gun" up and bring the cats in. *"Yes, your right Yuseph."* Hey, Nika, thank you.

After hanging up, I opened a pack of "Morittas." As I inhale. I start to think, *"Maybe man can never be free because they're weak, corrupt, worthless, and restless. The people believe in authority. They've grown tiered of waiting. "Man has been programmed for slavery. He alone who owns the youth, gains the future."* It's almost funny, that The Victor will never be asked, if he told the truth.

The Leftist, they have their ways, as they have their sayings, "Death, is the solution to all problems. No man, equals no problem." That sick, "democratic socialist," Subam took our guns first. Then went on to take our ideas. *"You see."* Subam said in a state run broadcast, *"Idea's are more powerful than gun's, we would not let men have gun's. Why should we let them have ideas?"* As I continued marking some points on my notes, I sent my girlfriend, "Lisa" a little "heart text."

I'm about ready but since I'm not due to speak for, I looked down at my watch, I have another hour. I'll have to kill some time. I head for the lunch room, to grab a "bite." As I returned with a good sized taco and shot glass of vodka, my cell "rang." Hello? *"Greetings Adama, it's Birdman."* Is something wrong? *"No, I just wanted to say goodbye. Just know that your fight has meaning."* Why are you saying this Birdman?

After Birdman hung up, I had a weird feeling in my gut. This wasn't typical of Birdman. He may have been working as a "Cheka" but that was just a "front." Even still, I want to double check, so I give Nika a call. Hey, Nika. I just wanted to check in with you. I received a call, so tell me, is it still raining? *"Nothing but rain Yuseph."* Okay great and Nika, I'm sorry about Natalia. After Nika and I got off the phone, I took a moment to reflect on, what I was doing and about those who were lost.

"Natalia has been on the "fronts" of this fight, since the beginning. I know she's "presumably" dead. After that failed attempt, to rescue her from Subam's compound, I think about her as well as back to my brother Ivan. He was the first soldier down in a fight. We have been "greatly" losing for the last eight years now." I continued going over my notes, just one more time.

As I finish off my bottle of vodka, I reach into my now empty pack of cigarettes. As I smoked, I'm not nervous, I just hope by doing this I am making a difference. Counting down the minutes before I speak, I walked out to meet a crowd. As I addressed them, I thanked them for their bravery for being here. *"Thank you. You're the fight. You're the last stand against tyranny. I would like to read for all of you, one of my favorite poems by Rudyard Kipling."*

"As I pass through my incarnations in every age and race, I make my proper prostrations to the Gods of the Market Place. Peering through reverent fingers I watch them flourish and fall, And the Gods of the Copybook Headings, I notice, outlast them all. We were living in trees when they met us. They showed us each in turn That Water would certainly wet us, as Fire would certainly burn: But we found them lacking in Uplift, Vision and Breadth of Mind, So we left them to teach the Gorillas while we followed the March of Mankind. We moved as the Spirit listed. They never altered their pace, Being neither cloud nor wind-borne like the Gods of the Market Place, But they always caught up with our progress, and presently word would come That a tribe had been wiped off its icefield, or the lights had gone out in Rome.

With the Hopes that our World is built on they were utterly out of touch, They denied that the Moon was Stilton; they denied she was even Dutch; They denied that Wishes were Horses; they denied that a Pig had Wings; So we worshipped the Gods of the Market Who promised these beautiful things. When the Cambrian measures were forming, They promised perpetual peace. They swore, if we gave them our weapons, that the wars of the tribes would cease. But when we disarmed They sold us and delivered us bound to our foe,

And the Gods of the Copybook Headings said: "Stick to the Devil you know." On the first Feminian Sandstones we were promised the Fuller Life (Which started by loving our neighbor and ended by loving his wife) Till our women had no more children and the men lost reason and faith, And the Gods of the Copybook Headings said: "The Wages of Sin is Death." In the Carboniferous Epoch we were promised abundance for all, By robbing selected Peter to pay for collective Paul; But, though we had plenty of money, there was nothing our money could buy, And the Gods of the Copybook Headings said: "If you don't work you die."

Pausing Half way through, I noticed "Birdman" in the crowd. As I thought to myself, *"He should not be here..."* With that thought, everything went to darkness...

29

IVAN VALENTIN'S STORY
PART 3

Laying in filth, at the bottom of the sewer, I'm captured. After "Subam's police force" got me out, of that God awful stench filled sewer, I received the beating of a lifetime. Subam was elected in January. It's now only, two months later and I'm being taken off to one of Subam's prisons to die. After cuffing me, one of the police officers busted me across the mouth with his flashlight. Breaking my nose as well as knocking my "front teeth out."

Once inside the "patrol car," one of Subam's "Loyal Dog's" asked me, "Was it worth it?" looking directly into his eye's, I answered. Yes, and no matter what you do, won't change that. "Well, we shall test that theory, Mr. Valentin." After the second officer entered the passenger side, my journey into certain unimaginable pain, most certainly followed, by death began...

Subam's policemen talked among themselves for some time, before the one sitting in the passenger's seat, turned towards my direction and started speaking. You're a sick fuck. Your little stunt caused the deaths of 12 friends of mine. I can't wait until I see you. You're going to be in so much pain, you'll be "begging, for death." You thought that, what? We wouldn't find you? You didn't actually think, that this would cause any problems for our government, did you? Seriously, fucking terrorist, you "Right Wing nut," what do you think? All you did, was scar the families of 12 good men. Men that had done nothing wrong other than showed up to work. I sat there saying nothing. As I watched him, I spit blood from my mouth, onto "the upholstery."

71

As the patrol car stopped at a red light. That same officer whom directed his attention to me moments ago, turned again but this time, to beat the shit out of me, with his night stick. He violently struck me, over and over. First jamming his night stick into my stomach. Then, he just started to unload swing, after swing. After being beaten to a bloody mess, my ribs feel broken. As it's hard to breathe, blood was all over the back seat. I don't want to but feel myself blacking out.

I awoke once, to see both of the officers. The patrol car stopped. The door of the back seat open, almost as if they were upside down. I watched, as they were talking and laughing. Suddenly, as if noticed, one of the officers looked down at me. I heard him say, "He's starting to come to..." Before closing the door, one of them asked, "Will you tell him?" I woke up off and on throughout the rest of the ride. I would see blurred images of the two police, before blacking out. After what actually felt like days, was probably only "40 minutes," tops. The two officers dragged me out of the back seat. My knees scrapping the concrete, as we came to a big wooden door. Hanging above, there was a huge "American flag," with Subam's face on it.

The doors opened as I heard the voice of a German women. "He is not dead, I hope?" I heard her asking the police officers. "No," They replied, "he's just been, "broken in a bit." Good. She said. They continued dragging me through a long hall until reaching a metal door. After throwing me in, the German woman said, "Don't worry, baby. I will be there soon, to take care of you." She then slammed the metal door, making a huge noise, that rang my ears.

Hours pass, as I waited for the worst. The silence alone was torture as I anticipated, what was to come. The door opened. I seen the figure of a man. He filled the door as he walked in, a nurse walked behind, pushing a tray. Covering the tray, were many tools and medical devices. Without wasting time, he turned to the woman. As she handed him a drill, he giggled with pleasure, with the noise of the drill in his hand's.

Walking over to me, laying there, he bent over pushing the power drill "through my knee." As I screamed out in pain, he said, "Don't worry. It only gets worse from here." The woman who had brought in the tray came over to me. She put her hand's around my shoulder's, as if to "comfort me." She began speaking to me. "You poor sweet baby. It hurts, yes? Don't cry. I am here with you." She began kissing me with her tongue, licking the blood from my mouth.

The man took my left hand, as he counted. "Inny, Mini, Minnie, moe." he cut my ring finger, completely off. As blood sprayed his face, he took a welding torch and burned the wound closed. As he did, she stuffed a rag down my throat. "Bite down, you see…" He told me. "It's constitutionalist" like you, that are a waste of human existence. Why couldn't you just accept progress, Mr. Valentin?" As I gagged on the rag, I heard him telling the German nurse, that "my mouth should be sealed up."

As she stood up, she fixed her skirt by pulling it down. She then said, "Yes doctor, I go to get supplies." He looked down at me saying, "She's a special kind of treat, isn't she?" I looked up at this beast panting. Fuck you and your transvestite! He simply grinned. As he turned to walk out, "We will return, Mr. Valentin." As the metal door again slammed shut, I collapsed.

Laying on the cold cement floor, it was almost as if "time froze." My entire body was in pain. My head felt numb to the touch. I felt a breeze. Not knowing where it was coming from, I picked my head up, trying in vane, to look around. My head then felt hitting the hard floor. After more than an hour must have passed, I tried bringing myself to my feet. As I "clumsily" stood, I looked around. Bringing my attention over to the tray, still sitting near the door.

Stumbling as I make my way over, I thought to myself, *"If I can get a weapon… No."* I then thought, *"I need to try and find another way out. I need to find where that breeze is coming from."* I stumbled to a corner in the room. Looking up, I see a ventilation shaft. I moved back to the tray, trying not to fall. I need a wire or a knife, that will do the trick. As I finally made it to the tray, the big metal door swung open. "Hello, mein boy." It was a "Cheka."

"Oh God." As he walked in, I fell to the floor. Walking in, he smiled and said, "You're up on your own. Very good mein freund." With that, he stabbed me with a small knife. The knife went through my right hand. "Now, be still."

He said. "Just, be still." Holding my hand as it bled, he walked over to the table, picking up scissors. "Now, let's begin." He grabbed my face, "I want to see if you can smile." He cuts me with the scissors, from my bottom lip, across to my cheek. Blood was everywhere, as he said, "Now, tell me, is there resistance?" *I couldn't speak. I couldn't breath.* I thought, *"Am I dying?"* as I blacked out.

I awoke to the sound of loud music. Too loud, to understand. I tried to move, until I realized, I was strapped down to a steel chair. I could see my reflection, in a big wall mirror, in front of me. *"A two-way mirror."* I thought. Sitting in the chair, my hands strapped down, a woman walked in.

"Hello Mr. Valentin, I have been told about you. Do you know how long, you have been with us?" I replied, "Why haven't you just killed me yet?" She smiled. I yelled, "Kill me! Kill me!" She walked over to me. She was dressed in a black, transparent gown. Underneath I could see that she was completely naked. "I love my men all tied up." She said, as she took out pliers. She began pulling at my finger nails. As I screamed, she started caressing herself.

"It's extremely exciting, isn't it, Mr. Valentin?" Fuck you, whore! Just kill me! "God, I'm becoming so wet." She said, while ripping out my finger nail. "You're almost ready to die, Mr. Valentin. You're going to be famous. Only, not for the reasons you would have liked." Kill me! I continued to yell. Just FUCKING, KILL ME! "In time yes, you will die. I can easily end your pain now. Please, let me." She moaned, as her voice trembled, she began rubbing between her leg's. Her thigh's becoming increasingly wet. Her mouth then partially opened as she bit down on her bottom lip. I replied, Do it! Yes! Fucking kill, me! "Is there any others, like you?" As she asked this question, her breathing became heavy.

My thoughts quickly went to "protecting my comrades." No. I answered. "Are you sure, no one else? Maybe someone, close to you, that may share your idea's?" She moaned while rubbing her clit, in a circular motion. No, nothing of that at all. I am alone. Now please, just let me die. She then started moaning, even stronger as she touched herself. "I'm going to cum Mr. Valentin!" She then asked, "Do you want a taste one last time before you go?" Rubbing her fingers across my face, I replied, "Your pussy tastes like shit."

Grabbing me by the back of my head, she pulled my head down. As she pulled, she lifted her gown, pushing my face as close as she could, to her aroused vagina. Her entire body shaking, she screamed as she erupted in pleasure. Her vagina then squirted, spraying all over my face, leaving me covered in her juice's. She then knocked on the two-way mirror. In doing so, two men walked in. "Prepare him for execution." She ordered them. The two officers took time to clean me up, as well to bandage my fingers and stitch my cheek together.

I was dressed in a white "jump suit" and given a cigarette. I asked calmly, "How long have I really, been here?" The officer answered, as he lit my cigarette. "Well, you've been here in sandstone corrections for about, eight days." Sand stone? I asked. "Yeah Mate, you're in Washington DC." How long have I been in custody? "Don't know mate, maybe three, four months. Didn't Madam Killian tell you?" No… "Well Mate, finish up the "fag." You're about to be "famous."

The two officers marched me over to a wall. I knew what this was. As I stood against the wall, I seen rows of soldiers. Their eye's were intense, as they stared at me, with their "riffles in hand." "Any last words?" Giving the sieg heil salute, I took a deep breath as I screamed, "Death to Subam! Death to the American government! Death to all who follow!" As I gave them the sieg heil salute, I heard, "Ready, aim, fire!" With that, bullet after bullet, "ripped" through my body. As I fell to the ground, all I could see was red.

30
CHRISTINE PAW'S STORY PART 3
IT WASN'T EXATLY HOW I THOUGHT

As Rave continued kissing me, he ripped the shirt I was wearing, freeing my breast. So wrapped up, I didn't care about the consequences. Molly, her face filled with rage, began yelling at the top of her lungs. Yelling at Rave and I. Quickly, I covered myself, wanting to apologies. I went to Molly. She slapped me across my face. Crying, I left the room knowing that soon, I would likely be back out on my own. I could hear them yelling for the longest time. Then it went silent. I waited before going out to check. Entering the living room, *"The scene of the crime."* I thought to myself.

I see molly sitting next to Rave. Her hand, gently rubbing his erected "manhood." Clearly surprised at this sudden change. Are you guys okay? I asked. Molly stood up. I was nervous as she walked towards me, considering what happened last time. Molly leaned in, putting her hand's on my face. She said, "I'm sorry." As she kissed me. "Come sit down with us." I heard from Rave.

I walked over to him. As he watched me, he slowly "masturbated." I nervously sat down, putting my hand over his as he touched himself. Licking my lips, I leaned in to suck him. Just then, I felt something. It was Molly. She stabbed me. As I fell with the blade, still in my spine, I found myself unable to move. I look over at Rave as if to say, "Help me" but he's laughing. Molly then kicks me in the stomach saying, "We're gonna have fun with you. See Rave, she's a whore, just like the others." I know sis, I know that. You're right. "So Rave, go put this bitch with the others." *Others?* I thought, with horror.

As rave dragged me away, he took me to a door that was opened and looked dark inside. After pushing me in, he turned on the light, I see women with "terrorized" looks in their eye's as they were in cages. Their body's cut and bruised. I wanted to scream yet, I was "paralyzed with fear." Before turning off the lights, rave said, "See ya later ladies and be nice to your new roomie." He then closed the door.

31

DIEGO'S FINAL ACT

It's been two months now, since my "daring escape." I've been living on the Streets, finding shelter wherever I can. I've noticed, while trying to "survive," that It's almost "funny" the way women are. They're always so careful during the day but have no problem walking around nearly "nude," at 2 o'clock in the morning, in front of their windows. It's also interesting how easy it is to spot a "single women." Most single women keep their bedroom windows open. They also seem more likely to have cat's.

I've been sleeping in gutters, looking over my shoulder for so long now. I don't even know the man I used to be. As I walk through the empty streets, among the other street people, I'm doing my best to blend in. When a police officer passes. *"I must have given him a "look."* As he looked at me, "Excuse me!" I heard, as I kept walking. As he kept pace behind me, I started running. As I ran, he pulled out his pistol. I felt my bones "snap," with the loud "bang." I felt my body go "numb." As I fell on the wet concrete, the last words I hear, "Why did you run, bum?" He didn't even know who I was. With that, he unloaded his pistol into my back.

CHAPTER 32

"As I report to you live on the ground, I can tell you it's bloody exciting what one would only think could exist, in a sci-fi film has happened. We are about to make contact with some sort of craft or beings outside of our known "reality." As I listened to the "News Reports," I was both excited and terrified at the idea. Reports kept coming in from America telling them to "remain indoors," while the "glorious Subam," assist the matter. I watched, hoping these beings were hostile. "Hopefully…" I thought. "They'll kill the "Glorious Subam.""

Today isn't the only time I've felt fear. I remember the day my mother was killed. "Subam's police" kicked in our door, "shooting" my mom. Caught by surprise, she was "shot 14 times." Save for the "fact I myself was not home," I would surely be dead and now, I watch this craft. This ship from another world and only "hope, it brings death" to Subam as well as all whom follow him. I hate that bastard Subam. I was "ten years old" when first my mother, then later my father, was killed by his "goons." I grew up on the run before my father's "murder." My father got me out of this "lost country." I grew up in "Russia" and now my dream's of Subam's death, may finally come true, for wishing. I stayed up, watching the news broadcast for as long as "possible," before falling asleep next to the TV.

I awoke to "screams" and loud "bangs." Looking outside, I gasped. "They're here." The ships over America's sky's, are now in Russia's as well. Fear struck me, as soldier's fired up at the two large crafts with no avail. The two crafts broke into four, shooting out "multiple rays," turning the soldiers to dust and their vehicles to liquid. "We're all going to die." I thought, as "I broke down in tears." I hit the floor in fear just as my neighbor came to my door "screaming."

"Adriana! Adriana! Let me in!" Climbing to my feet I opened the door. He was bleeding. I asked him, "What happened?" He just said, "They're not like us." Before passing out… I went to my window, as I seen "silver creatures with long tails," running in the streets, attacking the people. Police had no effect using their guns, to shoot whatever they are. Then a car hit my down stairs neighbor's house.

The people inside the car tried fleeing but the creatures soon "struck them." Long needles from out of their arms, penetrated their bodies, killing them before they could fall. I've never seen anything like this. I'm so scared. I don't know what if anything I can do? As I moved back from the window, I felt fear as I heard "tapping," coming from my ceiling. It was at that moment, when I looked up, something grabbed my leg. Terrified, I started screaming. Then I've seen them. Long and silver. I stood there frozen in fear. I couldn't move as if the creature couldn't see. It began inspecting me.

33
CHARLES ADAMA JOHNSON'S STORY

I've been living in this "New World Order," since before Subam. Subam has been dominating our existence, for five years now. He was elected, five years ago today. In January 2020, the world didn't "change." He just made it more honest. The left had been wanting this for so long. Subam just had the "balls" to get it done. Like the leftist "denial of natural climate change." I don't think humanity was pumping carbon dioxide emissions into the skies, around the first second or third ice age, that our planet has had or that dark-age hot period but the "leftist" and their "wicked ways," silence basic information in order to "feed us their perverted falsehoods."

So, I wasn't surprised to see Subam win. Fucking "useful idiots." As best said by "Lenin." I feel I've lived long enough. These "Americans," will never wake up. I have decided tonight, I will "kill myself." I've never had a thought such as this but this new, "liberal utopia?" A man like myself, cannot live. I prefer the "freedom of death," then a "life of servitude."

Joseph Adama

34
CARL'S STORY
THE SOLDIER

I served in "The Great War." I was at one point, a true believer in this "once great country." I fought what was later called, "Boomers War." I protected my country against "Korean foes." I lost my hand without regrets, "for my country and for my brother's" but now, that man who so "proudly fought" only eleven years ago, is no more. My country is gone. My people are no longer "my people" nor can they call themselves "American." Those courageous men, whom served in "The Great War," were "heroes." The men that sacrificed everything during the war of "Stalingrad," like my grandfather, they're heroes but these so called Americans are nothing more than "sheep," getting ready for slaughter.

In 1963 John F. Kennedy, my fathers favorite President, defended our nation in the war against Russia. Later known as the war of Stalingrad. We fought against "Communism" for what purpose? We fought the "Islamic State of Mexico," for what purpose? To have the leftist blame Islamic fascism, on "climate change?" We fought, we died, trying to preserve our founder's "vision." For what? To just casually hand our Nation over to a "tyrant?" No, I can't accept this cowardice "anti-free," anti-prosperous, welfare state, of "sheep" as they "Bah Bah Bah" to their "savior," their "precious government." I shall strike against tyranny.

35
JOSEPH & IVAN'S STORY
THE BEGENNING

Hello, my name is "Joseph Frankie Johnson Adama." I first met "Ivan Valentin" in the spring of 2010. We shared the same "neighborhood." I first encountered Ivan, due to his "out spoken views." The man "had" balls. He was wearing a shirt expressing his views against then, Republican President Boomer's stance, on rape victims. Right as we got to talking, we realized how much we did have in common. He was eighteen and just "starting out" in the world, so to speak. His views on Americans, I myself didn't yet share.

He told me that Americans were slowly but surly, allowing themselves to be "fucked" by their "government," in return for "welfare and food stamps." The US citizens was gladly handing over more and more "rights." I told him, "I too hate President Boomer but Americans aren't stupid to the point of disavowing the constitution." We agreed as well as we disagreed at the end.

As I sit here, months after "Subam" took control of "my former country," I am stuck "thinking about how right he was." He said, "The Senate would be dissolved, along with the courts." I told him, "that would never happen." After Subam took power, I told him that I'd write. I will use my words to wake up the "sleeping." It's been a few months now and "Ivan's execution," still plays out in my head. Ivan Valentin, I'll make sure your "death means something." I've seen that which follows Subam's rule, will end.

Subam

END

Subam

A special thanks to JV & Colombia. I must also thank my brother, Joseph
Adama, for all the things, we have been through with writing.

Sincerely, Ivan

First of all, I must give my thanks and respect to Ivan Valentin, who has gone above and beyond the call, to insure that our book be brought to you the readers. If not for him, putting the time into my Book Subam Subam 2020, It would likely still be sitting on a shelf. For Ivan had been the one to bring my work, my vision of a world gone mad with leftist world order to the readers. As he was the one I have had edit, upload and take the time to look through my work, to insure that Subam would be all it could be. I'd also like to thank my mom. As well as all those who read and enjoy my Book. Thank you for your support.

Writer of Subam. Joseph F. Adama

Joseph Adama

Subam